3D POP-UP CARD

BEGINN

A straightforward card-making guidebook on how to create a stunning 3D pop-up card for beginners

SARA GRISHAM

Table of Contents

CHAPTER ONE

INTRODUCTION

3D pop-up cards are a form of a greeting card that opens to reveal a three-dimensional effect. They have a major picture or design that "pops up" from the card, which is usually in the shape of a sculpture or architectural building. Pop-up design features are often constructed utilizing a mix of paper engineering techniques such as cutting, folding, and layering.

3D pop-up cards are suitable for a range of events, including birthdays, and holidays, and for expressing thanks or devotion. They are frequently constructed of high-quality paper and artistically decorated, giving them a one-of-a-kind and memorable method to express a message.

3D pop-up cards have grown in popularity in recent years, with several firms specializing in the development and marketing of these one-of-a-kind cards. They come in a range of styles, from whimsical and fun to beautiful and refined, and may be tailored to the recipient's personality and hobbies.

HISTORY OF 3D POP-UP CARD

The origins of 3D pop-up cards may be traced back to the early nineteenth century, when "metamorphoses," a type of moveable book, were popular in Europe. These books included pictures that could be moved and manipulated, giving the impression of depth and movement.

By the mid-nineteenth century, pop-up book technology had

evolved, and artists and paper engineers began to experiment with utilizing pop-up components in greeting cards. The first documented 3D pop-up card was made in the late 1800s, and these cards grew in popularity over the next several decades.

In the mid-20th century, the rise of mass-produced greeting cards led to a decline in the popularity of 3D pop-up cards. However, in recent years, there has been a resurgence of interest in these unique and intricate cards, with many people seeking out handmade or custom-made pop-up cards as a special way to express their feelings.

Today, 3D pop-up cards continue to be a popular form of greeting cards, with many artists and companies specializing in their creation. They are widely available in a variety of styles, themes, and designs, and are often used for special occasions such as birthdays, holidays, and anniversaries.

TYPES OF 3D POP-UP CARDS

There are many different types of 3D pop-up cards, each with its own unique design and features. Some of the most common types of 3D pop-up cards include:

Architectural pop-up cards: These cards feature iconic buildings or architectural structures that "pop up" from the card when opened. Examples include the Eiffel Tower, the Colosseum, and the Taj Mahal.

Nature pop-up cards: These cards feature images of plants, animals, and other elements from nature.

Examples include flowers, trees, and birds.

Sculptural pop-up cards: These cards feature intricate sculptures that "pop up" from the card when opened. Examples include geometric shapes, abstract designs, and complex machinery.

Character pop-up cards: These cards feature characters from popular movies, TV shows, or comic books that "pop up" from the card when opened. Examples include Mickey Mouse, Superman, and Spider-Man.

Holiday-themed pop-up cards: These cards are designed to be used for specific holidays, such as Christmas, Valentine's Day, or Easter. They often feature holiday-themed images and designs that "pop up" from the card when opened.

Personalized pop-up cards: These cards are custom-made to feature a specific message or image. They can be designed to include a person's name, a special date, or a favorite photo.

There are many other types of 3D pop-up cards as well, and new designs and styles are constantly being created by artists and paper engineers. Regardless of the type, 3D pop-up cards are a unique and special way to convey a message and make a lasting impression.

3D POP-UP CARD MAKING

Making a 3D pop-up card is a fun and creative project that involves paper engineering and a little bit of imagination. Here are the steps to make a basic 3D pop-up card:

Gather materials: You will need a piece of cardstock for the base of the card, a ruler, a pencil, scissors, a glue stick, and decorative paper or patterned paper for the pop-up elements.

Cut the cardstock: Cut the cardstock to the desired size for the base of the card. The card should be folded in half, so make sure it is large enough to accommodate the pop-up elements when opened.

Draw the pop-up elements: Draw the pop-up elements on the

decorative paper. This could be anything from a simple shape, such as a heart or star, to a more complex design, such as a building or animal. Be sure to think about the size and placement of the pop-up elements, as well as how they will fit on the card when folded.

Cut out the pop-up elements: Carefully cut out the pop-up elements using scissors. Make sure to leave a small margin around the elements to allow for easy folding.

Assemble the pop-up elements: Fold the pop-up elements along the lines you drew, using a ruler to create crisp folds. Glue the elements together to create a 3D structure.

Attach the pop-up elements to the card: Apply glue to the back of the pop-up elements and attach them to the card, making sure they are positioned correctly when the card is closed. Allow the glue to dry completely.

Decorate the card: Decorate the outside and inside of the card as desired. You could use markers, stickers, or other decorative elements to make the card even more special.

Fold the card: Fold the card in half and secure it closed. Your 3D pop-up card is now complete!

Making a 3D pop-up card takes a little bit of patience and creativity, but the end result is a unique and special piece of art that can be given to someone special. With a little practice, you can create more complex pop-up designs and make even more intricate cards.

CHAPTER TWO

HOW TO MAKE A 3D POP-UP BIRTHDAY CARD

Making a 3D pop-up birthday card is a fun and creative way to celebrate someone's special day. Here are the steps to make a simple 3D pop-up birthday cake card:

Gather materials: You will need a piece of cardstock for the base of the card, a ruler, a pencil, scissors, a glue stick, and decorative paper for the pop-up elements. You will also need patterned paper or decorative elements, such as stickers or washi tape, to decorate the card.

Cut the cardstock: Cut the cardstock to the desired size for the base of the card. The card should be folded in half, so make sure it is large enough to accommodate the pop-up cake when opened.

Draw the pop-up cake: Draw the basic shape of a birthday cake on a piece of decorative paper. You could draw a simple layer cake or a more elaborate tiered cake. Think about the size and placement of the cake, as well as how it will fit on the card when folded.

Cut out the pop-up cake: Carefully cut out the pop-up cake using scissors. Make sure to leave a small margin around the cake to allow for easy folding.

Assemble the pop-up cake: Fold the pop-up cake along the lines you drew, using a ruler to create crisp folds. Glue the cake together to create a 3D structure.

Attach the pop-up cake to the card: Apply glue to the back of the pop-up cake and attach it to the card, making sure it is positioned correctly when the card is closed. Allow the glue to dry completely.

Decorate the card: Decorate the outside and inside of the card as desired. You could use markers, stickers, or other decorative elements to make the card even more special. Consider writing a birthday message on the inside of the card.

Fold the card: Fold the card in half and secure it closed. Your 3D pop-up birthday cake card is now complete!

With a little creativity, you can make a variety of different pop-up birthday cards, such as a pop-up balloon card or a pop-up present card. Just use your imagination and have fun!

GATHERING MATERIALS

When making a 3D pop-up card, it is important to gather the right materials to ensure a successful outcome. Here is a list of common materials used in 3D pop-up card-making:

Cardstock: This is the base of your card and is used to provide stability and structure. Look for heavy-duty cardstock that is sturdy enough to hold the pop-up elements. You can choose any color or pattern that you like.

Decorative paper: This is used for the pop-up elements and can be any patterned or decorative paper that you like. It can be plain, patterned, or textured and can add visual interest to your card.

Scissors: You will need sharp scissors for cutting the cardstock and decorative paper. Choose a pair of scissors that are comfortable for you to use and that make clean cuts.

Ruler: A ruler is used to measure and score the cardstock and decorative paper. This will help you make precise cuts and folds.

Pencil: A pencil is used to draw the pop-up elements and make any necessary markings on the cardstock and decorative paper.

Glue stick: A glue stick is used to attach the pop-up elements to the cardstock. Choose a strong, clear-drying glue that will not wrinkle the paper.

Decorative elements: You can use a variety of decorative elements to enhance your cards, such as stickers, washi tape, markers, or sequins. Use your imagination to create a unique and special card.

These are the basic materials that you will need to make a 3D pop-up card. With these materials, you can create a wide variety of pop-up designs and make cards that are truly one-of-a-kind.

CUTTING THE CARD STOCK

When cutting the cardstock for your 3D pop-up birthday card, it is important to be precise and accurate. Here are some tips for cutting the cardstock:

Measure and mark the cardstock: Measure and mark the desired size of your card, making sure that it is large enough to accommodate the pop-up element when the card is folded. Use a ruler and pencil to make straight, clean lines.

Cut the cardstock: Cut the cardstock along the lines you marked, using sharp scissors. Be sure to make clean, straight cuts and to keep the edges of the cardstock straight.

Fold the cardstock: Once you have cut the cardstock to the desired size, fold it in half along the centerline to create the card base.

Make sure the fold is crisp and straight.

Score the cardstock: If your pop-up element will require multiple folds, use a ruler and a pencil to score the cardstock along the lines where you will be making folds. This will make it easier to create sharp, precise folds when you assemble the pop-up element.

Test the fold: Before attaching the pop-up element to the card, test the fold to make sure that the pop-up element will sit correctly when the card is closed. Make any necessary adjustments before you attach the element to the card.

By following these tips, you can ensure that the cardstock for your 3D pop-up birthday card is cut accurately and precisely, which will result in a beautiful and professional-looking card.

DRAWING THE POP-UP CAKE

Drawing the pop-up cake for your 3D pop-up birthday card can be a fun and creative process. Here are some steps for drawing a simple pop-up cake design:

Sketch the cake: Use a pencil to sketch a simple cake shape on a piece of decorative paper. You can start with a basic round shape for the cake and add a few wavy lines to represent the frosting.

Cut out the cake: Once you are satisfied with your cake sketch, carefully cut it out with sharp scissors. Be sure to cut along the lines precisely to ensure that the cake will pop up properly when the card is opened.

Score and fold the cake: Use a ruler and a pencil to score the back of the cake along the center line. This will create a fold that will allow the cake to stand up when the card is opened. Fold the cake along the scored line and press down gently to create a crisp fold.

Attach the cake to the card: Apply glue to the back of the cake and attach it to the center of the card, making sure that the fold is aligned with the center of the card. Hold the cake in place until the glue dries.

By following these simple steps, you can create a fun and visual pop-up cake design for your 3D pop-up birthday card. You can also use this technique to create other pop-up elements, such as candles or presents, to add even more visual interest to your card.

CUTTING OUT THE POP-UP CAKE

Cutting out the pop-up cake for your 3D pop-up birthday card is an important step in the creation process. Here are some steps for cutting out the pop-up cake design:

Choose the right paper: Select a decorative paper that matches the color scheme of your card or adds a pop of color. Make sure that the paper is sturdy enough to hold the cake shape when the card is opened.

Sketch the cake: Use a pencil to sketch a simple cake shape on the decorative paper. You can start with a basic round shape for the cake and add a few wavy lines to represent the frosting.

Cut around the cake: Use sharp scissors to carefully cut around the cake sketch, following the lines precisely. Be sure to cut through both layers of the paper to create a clean edge.

Cut out the center of the cake: Use a craft knife or scissors to carefully cut out a small triangle-shaped piece from the center of the cake. This will allow the cake to pop up when the card is opened.

Trim any rough edges: Once you have cut out the cake, inspect the edges to make sure they are smooth and clean. Use scissors to trim any rough or uneven edges.

By following these simple steps, you can successfully cut out the pop-up cake design for your 3D pop-up birthday card. Remember to take your time and be precise with your cuts to ensure a professional and visually appealing result.

ASSEMBLING THE POP-UP CAKE

Assembling the pop-up cake for your 3D pop-up birthday card is an important step in the creation process. Here are some steps for assembling the pop-up cake design:

Prepare the card: Fold the cardstock in half to create the card base and make sure the fold is crisp and straight.

Attach the cake: Apply glue to the back of the cake and attach it to the center of the card, making sure that the cut-out triangle is facing up. Hold the cake in place until the glue dries.

Secure the cake: Use a small piece of tape or a tiny dot of glue to secure the bottom of the cut-out triangle to the inside of the card. This will help keep the cake in place when the card is opened.

Check the pop-up: Gently open the card and check to make sure that the cake pops up as desired. If the cake does not pop up, adjust the placement of the cut-out triangle or add a small piece of foam tape to help it pop up.

By following these simple steps, you can successfully assemble the pop-up cake design for your 3D pop-up birthday card. Remember to be patient and take your time to ensure that the cake pops up correctly and looks visually appealing.

ATTACHING THE POP-UP CAKE TO THE CARD

Attaching the pop-up cake to the card is an important step in creating your 3D pop-up birthday card. Here are some steps for attaching the pop-up cake to the card:

Apply glue: Apply a thin layer of glue to the back of the pop-up cake. Make sure that the glue is evenly spread and covers the entire back of the cake.

Align the cake: Hold the cake in place and align the center of the cake with the center of the card. Be sure to place the cake so that the cut-out triangle is facing up.

Adhere the cake: Carefully press the cake onto the card, making sure that it is securely attached. Hold the cake in place for a few seconds until the glue dries.

Check the placement: Gently open the card to check the placement of the pop-up cake. If the cake is not centered or does not pop up correctly, gently lift the cake and adjust the placement as needed.

By following these simple steps, you can successfully attach the pop-up cake to your 3D pop-up birthday card. Remember to take your time and be precise with the placement of the cake to ensure a visually appealing result.

DECORATING THE CARD

Decorating your 3D pop-up birthday card is the final step in the creation process and allows you to add your own personal touch to the card. Here are some steps for decorating your card:

Choose decorations: Select a variety of decorative elements such as stickers, ribbons, glitter, and buttons to add to your card. Make sure to choose items that complement the color scheme of the card and the pop-up cake design.

Decorate the card front: Start by decorating the front of the card. You can use stickers or cut-out shapes to create a festive design or use a pen or marker to write a personal message.

Decorate the inside: Turn the card over and decorate the inside as desired. You can add additional stickers, or drawings, or write a birthday message to the recipient.

Add finishing touches: Once the decorations are in place, add any final touches to the card. For example, you can tie a ribbon or bow around the card, add a sprinkle of glitter, or attach a button or charm to the card front.

By following these simple steps, you can successfully decorate your 3D pop-up birthday card and make it truly unique and special. Remember to have fun and be creative with your decorations to make the card truly special and memorable.

FOLDING THE 3D POP UP BIRTHDAY CARD

Folding the 3D pop-up birthday card is an important step in creating the card. Here are some steps for folding the card:

Start with a flat piece of cardstock: Lay the cardstock flat on a clean, flat surface.

Mark the center: Use a ruler to measure and mark the center of the cardstock.

Fold in half: Fold the cardstock in half along the marked center line, creasing it firmly.

Check the fold: Open the card and make sure that the fold is crisp and straight. If the fold is not straight, refold the card and make any necessary adjustments.

Repeat the process: Fold the card in half again in the same direction, creasing it firmly. This will create a smaller folded card that will serve as the base for your 3D pop-up design.

By following these simple steps, you can successfully fold your 3D pop-up birthday card and create the foundation for your pop-up design. Remember to take your time and make sure that the fold is straight and crisp for a visually appealing result.

CHAPTER THREE

TROUBLESHOOTING

Making a 3D pop-up card can be a fun and creative process, but it can also present some challenges. Here are some common problems that you may encounter while making your 3D pop-up card and how to troubleshoot them:

Pop-up design not popping up: If the pop-up design is not popping up correctly, it may be due to a weak pop-up mechanism. To fix this, try adding more glue to the base of the pop-up design or reinforcing the pop-up mechanism with a small piece of paper.

Uneven pop-up: If the pop-up design is not popping up evenly, it may be due to an uneven cut in the cardstock. To fix this, trim any uneven edges and make sure that the pop-up mechanism is centered on the card.

Collapsed pop-up: If the pop-up design collapses when the card is opened, it may be due to too much weight on the design or a weak pop-up mechanism. To fix this, try reducing the weight of the design or reinforcing the pop-up mechanism with a small piece of paper.

Poor adhesion: If the pop-up design is not adhering well to the card, it may be due to a lack of glue or a weak adhesive. To fix this, apply more glue to the back of the pop-up design or try a stronger adhesive such as double-sided tape.

By being aware of these common problems and knowing how to troubleshoot them, you can ensure that your 3D pop-up card turns out looking great. If all else fails, don't be afraid to start over and try again! Making 3D pop-up cards is a fun and creative process, and with some practice and patience, you'll be able to create beautiful and unique cards in no time!

HOW TO START A 3D POP-UP CARD-MAKING BUSINESS

Starting a 3D pop-up card-making business can be a fun and creative way to turn your passion for card-making into a profitable venture. Here are some steps to help you get started:

Conduct market research: Research the market to determine the demand for 3D pop-up cards and who your target market is. Look at the competition, pricing, and styles to get an idea of what you will be up against.

Create a business plan: Develop a detailed business plan that outlines your goals, target market, and marketing strategies. This plan will serve as a roadmap for your business and help guide your decision-making process.

Gather materials and equipment: You will need cardstock, scissors, glue, and other supplies for creating your cards. Consider purchasing a die-cutting machine or other specialized equipment to help streamline the production process.

Establish a brand: Develop a brand identity that includes a logo, color scheme, and other elements that will set you apart from the competition.

Set up a workspace: Choose a space in your home or rent a

studio where you can create your cards. Make sure the space is well-lit, organized, and equipped with all the necessary tools and supplies.

Market your business: Use social media, advertising, and other marketing strategies to promote your business and reach your target market. Consider participating in craft fairs and other events to showcase your cards and reach a wider audience.

Price your cards: Determine a pricing strategy for your cards based on your costs, the competition, and the market demand. Be sure to factor in the cost of materials, equipment, and labor when determining your prices.

By following these steps and continually refining your business practices, you can successfully start and grow your 3D pop-up card-making business. Good luck!

HOW TO ENSURE THE PROFITABILITY OF A 3D POP-UP CARD-MAKING BUSINESS

Ensuring the profitability of a 3D pop-up card-making business requires a combination of effective cost management, efficient production processes, and effective marketing strategies. Here are some tips to help you ensure the profitability of your business:

Keep costs low: Make sure to keep your costs low by buying materials in bulk, using cost-effective production methods, and avoiding unnecessary expenses.

Streamline production: Make sure to streamline your production process by using specialized equipment and efficient techniques to create your cards. The more efficient your production process, the more cards you can produce in less time, and the more profit you can make.

Focus on quality: Make sure to focus on quality and attention to detail in your cards. High-quality cards will command a higher price and generate more repeat business.

Market effectively: Use a variety of marketing strategies, including social media, advertising, and networking, to reach your target market and promote your cards. Consider offering discounts and promotions to encourage customers to buy.

Diversify your offerings: Consider offering a variety of different types of cards, including holiday cards, birthday cards, and special occasion cards, to reach a wider range of customers and generate more sales.

Monitor your finances: Keep track of your income and expenses, and regularly review your financial statements to ensure that you are making a profit. Make adjustments to your pricing and production processes as needed to maximize profitability.

By following these tips and continually monitoring and refining your business practices, you can ensure the profitability of your 3D pop-up card-making business and achieve success. Good luck!

FAQ

Here are some frequently asked questions about 3D pop-up card-making:

What materials do I need to make a 3D pop-up card?

You will need cardstock, scissors, glue, a cutting mat, a ruler, a bone folder, and a pen or pencil for drawing and cutting your card. You may also want to use a die-cutting machine or other specialized equipment to help streamline the production process.

How do I design a 3D pop-up card?

To design a 3D pop-up card, you will need to create a design for the pop-up mechanism, cut the cardstock to size, fold the card into its pop-up form, and decorate the card as desired. You can find templates and tutorials online to help guide you through the process.

Can I use different types of paper for my 3D pop-up cards?

Yes, you can use different types of paper for your 3D pop-up cards, including patterned paper, glitter paper, and specialty cardstock. However, it is important to choose sturdy and durable paper that will hold its shape and not bend or tear when the card is opened and closed.

What is the best way to attach the pop-up mechanism to the card base?

The best way to attach the pop-up mechanism to the card base is to use strong, clear-drying glue, such as double-sided tape or glue dots, to secure the mechanism in place. You can also use a combination of adhesive and ribbon or string to reinforce the connection and ensure that the pop-up mechanism stays securely in place.

How do I decorate my 3D pop-up cards?

You can decorate your 3D pop-up cards using a variety of techniques, including stamping, embossing, die-cutting, and adding embellishments such as stickers, rhinestones, and ribbons. The sky is the limit when it comes to decorating your cards, so get creative and have fun!

How can I make my 3D pop-up cards unique and stand out from others?

You can make your 3D pop-up cards unique by choosing interesting pop-up mechanisms, incorporating special techniques and materials, and decorating your cards with unique embellishments and designs. You can also try offering personalized or custom cards to help set your cards apart from others.

These are just a few of the frequently asked questions about 3D pop-up card making. With creativity, practice, and attention to detail, you can create beautiful and unique 3D pop-up cards that will be enjoyed by your friends and family.

CONCLUSION

In conclusion, making 3D pop-up cards is an enjoyable and rewarding craft that can bring joy to those who receive them and pride to those who create them. The skills and techniques covered in this book will provide you with a strong foundation to build upon and explore your own creative ideas. The possibilities for designing pop-up cards are virtually limitless, and the more you practice, the more confident and skilled you will become.

Remember that the most important aspect of this craft is having fun and letting your imagination soar. Don't be afraid to experiment and try new things. And, above all, enjoy the process! Whether you're making cards for special occasions, gifts, or simply for your own enjoyment, the end result will always be a unique and beautiful piece of art. So, keep practicing and creating, and never stop exploring the world of 3D pop-up card making.

THE END

Printed in Great Britain
by Amazon

40159418R00036